Wake Up to the World of Science

ARRANGING YOUR COLLECTION

B. Bornancin

Burke Books ►B LONDON ∗ TORONTO ∗ NEW YORK

First published in the English language 1
Revised and reprinted 1984
© Burke Publishing Company Limited 1
Translated and adapted from *Faisons des* ....
© Editions Fernand Nathan 1981

Acknowledgements

The publishers are grateful to Jennifer Dyke for preparing the text of this edition, and to the following for permission to reproduce copyright illustrations:
   Atlas-Photo, Bornancin, Boulet, Jacana, Labag, Puig. *Cover:* Labat.
The drawings are by Michel Janvier.

CIP data

Arranging your collection. – (Wake up to the world of science)
   1. Natural history   2. Collectors and collecting
   I. Bornancin, B.   II. Merigot, M.
   III. Faisons des collections. *English*   IV. Series
      500.9'075   QH61
   ISBN 0 222 00929 2
   ISBN 0 222 00930 6 Pbk

Burke Publishing Company Limited
Pegasus House, 116-120 Golden Lane, London EC1Y 0TL, England.
Burke Publishing (Canada) Limited
Registered Office: 20 Queen Street West, Suite 3000, Box 30, Toronto, Canada M5H 1V5.
Burke Publishing Company Inc.
Registered Office: 333 State Street, PO Box 1740, Bridgeport, Connecticut 06601, U.S.A.
Filmset in "Monophoto" Souvenir by Green Gates Studios Ltd., Hull, England.
Printed in the Netherlands by Deltaprint Holland.

CONTENTS

Dried flower and plant arrangements

Many plants or parts of plants can be kept with no special preparation at all. Beautiful flower arrangements can be made with dried grasses (a), while old branches covered with lichen, or curiously-shaped pieces of root make a very original decoration (b).

a

b

c

Cones

The fruits of trees such as the pine, the fir and the cypress are called **cones**, and the tree themselves are called **conifers**.

It is very easy to collect cones and varnish them, or paint them as in the photograph (c) on page 4. They can also be mounted, as in the photograph (right).

Here is a table to help you find the names of the trees which correspond to the various cones.

	If the fruit looks like:	the tree is:
	– a small **ball** made up of about 10 scales, each one looking like a large hob nail	**a cypress**
	– a **small** round cone, 2 to 4 cm long, and the tree loses its leaves in the winter	**a larch**
	– **typical pyramid-shaped cone**	
	3 to 6 cm ($\frac{3}{4}$ to $1\frac{1}{2}$ in) long	**a Scots Pine**
	4 to 7 cm ($1\frac{1}{2}$ to $2\frac{3}{4}$ in) long, and the scales have prickles	**a Shore Pine**
	– 6 to 10 cm ($2\frac{1}{4}$ to 4 in) long	**an Aleppo Pine**
	12 to 18 cm ($4\frac{3}{4}$ to 7 in) long	**a Maritime Pine**
	– **a cylinder** standing upright on the tree, and gradually losing its scales	**a fir tree**
	hanging downwards; keeps its scales	**a spruce**
	– a large **egg**, 6 to 13 cm ($2\frac{1}{4}$ to 5 in) long, with tight rows of scales which it loses progressively	**a cedar**

Dry fruits .

Fruits from trees in the park

Dried fruits are very plentiful on **trees,** on **shrubs** and on **grasses**. Always collect fruits which are completely ripe, and examine them carefully.

They can be arranged according to their shape, colour or size, or the place where they were collected.

Different types of dried fruits:

1 Follicles – rose bay, stercularia, hellebore.

2 Pods – pea, gorse.

3 Siliqua – wallflower.

4 Capsules – poppy, cana, tulip, iris, campion, snapdragon.

5 Achenes – acorn, chestnut, fruits of the ash and the maple.

6 Caryopsis – wheat.

7 Achene – salsify.

Classifying dry fruits

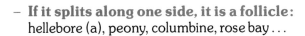

The fruit opens and releases several seeds

a

b

seeds

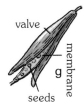

c

teeth

d

holes

e

cover

seeds

f

- **If it splits along one side, it is a follicle:**
  hellebore (a), peony, columbine, rose bay . . .

- **If it splits along two sides, it is a pod:**
  pea (b), bean, lucerne, and all other members of that family.

- **If there are several splits or holes, it is a capsule:**
  violet (c), primrose (d), poppy (e), pimpernel (f), tulip, iris, snapdragon, St John's wort . . .

valve

membrane

g

seeds

- **If it splits into two halves, separated by a fine membrane, it is a siliqua:**
  wallflower (g), honesty, cabbage, and all other members of that family.

The fruit does not open and contains only one seed

h

- **Grass seeds**
  wheat (h), oats, maize and all types of wild grasses, such as couch grass.

- **Fruits from trees and other plants** (achenes)
  acorns (i), chestnuts, hazelnuts, carrot (j) and parsley seeds.
  The fruits may be **winged** like those of the elm (k), the ash and the maple, or have **hairs** like those of the dandelion

i

j

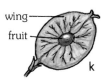

wing

fruit

k

Making a herbarium

1. Why make a herbarium?

Your herbarium will enable you to:
- collect many different kinds of **leaves** and classify them;
- compare **twigs and branches** at different times of the year (trees in your garden for example).
- see how **the flower changes into a fruit** in certain plants.
- gather together **plants which live in the same location** (meadow plants, or mountain plants for example).
- observe the **different flower families** etc.

2. How to make a herbarium

If you want to preserve the plants which you collect, there are a few simple rules you must follow. Otherwise you might be disappointed with the result.

Out of doors

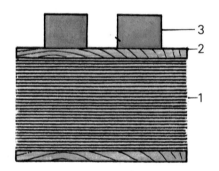

Choose a leafy twig and lay it between two sheets of newspaper.

Write down the date and the place it was collected; also the name of the plant, if you know it.

At home: make a press

- Place the twig **very flat** in a fresh fold of newspaper, together with all the relevant information.
- Place about ten of these folds of paper on a board (1) and cover with another piece of wood (2). Now put a heavy weight on top (3). A few telephone directories would be ideal.
- Put this **press** in a dry, well-ventilated spot.
- Check every three or four days. If the papers are a little damp, replace them with new ones.

Take particular care with flowers. You will find they generally lose colour as they dry. But you can improve this by **ironing them;** place the flower between two sheets of blotting paper and go over it with a warm iron (medium setting).

- When the plants are **completely dry**, (after two or three weeks), stick them onto a sheet of thick paper or board with pieces of clear adhesive tape or, better still, a few dabs of glue. Write on the paper, or on a label, **the name, the date and the place where they were collected.**
- Put your papers in a stiff folder or cardboard box, and protect them from dust and damp. In this way they will keep for years.

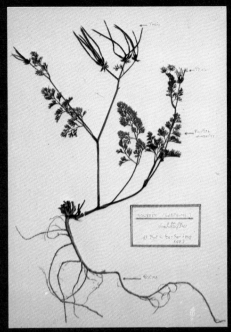

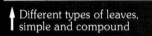

↑ Different types of leaves,
simple and compound

↑ Various weeds
with their roots

Plant galls

Leaves sometimes have curious little scabs, spikes and bobbles on them. These are caused by **parasites**. The plant attacked by a parasite often reacts by producing a new sort of organism called a gall. If you open one up, you will often find an insect larva, or a very small spider inside.

a

b

c

You can easily collect these galls by putting the affected leaves in a herbarium. The larger ones can be kept with no special preparation.

d

e

a Red pointed gall on the lime
b Hairy gall on the wild rose
c An insect larva inside the wild rose gall
d Gall on a poplar leaf
e Galls on oak leaves

A few common galls

1. On the oak:

– **Round greenish-yellow gall,** 1 to 2 cm ($\frac{3}{8}$ to $\frac{3}{4}$ in) in diameter. Very hard. Found near the buds.

– **"Artichoke" gall,** which causes the bud scales to become enormous.

– **Small yellow spots,** about 0.5 cm ($\frac{3}{16}$ in) in diamete found on the underside of the leaves.

– A **red cherry-like gall,** on the underside of the leaf.

2. On the beech:

– **"Orange-pip" gall,** about 0.5 to 1 cm ($\frac{3}{16}$ to $\frac{3}{8}$ in) long on the upper surface of the leaf.

3. On the poplar

– The gall produces a **coiling of the leaf-stalk.**

4. On the lime sycamore

– a gall in the form of **small, red spikes** (a)

5. On the wild rose

– the "bedeguar" or rose-gall. A **hairy gall** 2 to 5 cm ($\frac{3}{4}$ to 2 in) in diameter, in the angle of a bud (b)

– a **round gall** on the surface of the leaves.

Collecting insects

It is not unusual to find dead insects during a walk in the countryside. If you do it would be a good time to start an **entomological** collection.

If the insects have only been dead for a short time (one or two days at the most), their legs, wings and antennae will still be pliable, and they can be prepared immediately.

But if the insects have been dead for a long time, their legs, wings and antennae will be very brittle and they must be handled with care. You will have to "soften" them again.

1. Softening

Take a preserving jar and put in a layer of fine sand about 4 cm (1½ in) thick. Dampen it slightly and put a couple of mothballs at the bottom. Wrap the insects in tissue paper, put them in the jar, and put on the lid (1). Small insects will be ready in 24 hours, larger ones in 48 hours.

1.

2. Preparation

Gather together the following materials (2):

– lengths of transparent tape (a)
– long, fine pins (b)
– headed pins (c)
– a needle mounted on a handle (d or f). You can make one yourself by attaching a needle firmly to a small stick of wood.
– a pair of eyebrow- or stamp-tweezers (e)
– a display board for coleoptera (beetles, etc.)
– a display board for butterflies

2.

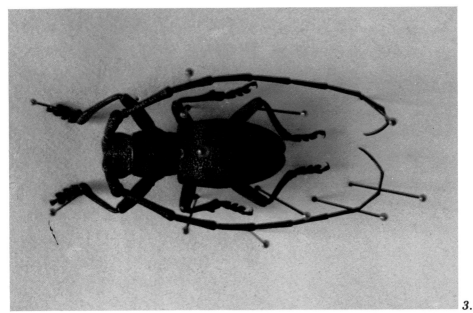

3.

Preparing the insects

Insects whose wings should not be spread out
(beetles, chafers, etc.)
– Stick a pin through the insect about a third of the way up the right-hand wing-case.
– Place it on the display board (a piece of polystyrene about 2 cm – $\frac{3}{4}$ in – thick would be ideal).
– Arrange the legs and antennae symmetrically, and pin them in position, as in the photograph.
– Leave to dry (3).

Insects whose wings should be spread out
(mantis, crickets, butterflies, etc.)
– Stick a pin through the thorax and fix it down the centre of the display-board (a).
– With the help of the needle with a handle, gently spread out the upper wings. Keep them in position with the lengths of clear tape (b).
– Now spread out the lower wings (c). Keep them in position with clear tape as well (d).
– Arrange the antennae and leave to dry for two weeks. (4).

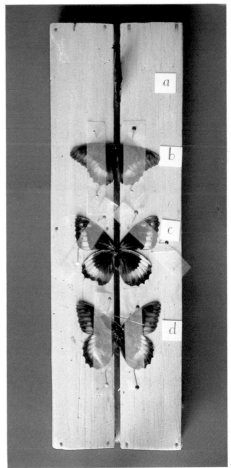

4.

How to store your insects

Choose **boxes with well-fitting lids,** transparent or otherwise. Line the bottom with polystyrene so that the pins will stick in easily.

Place a **moth-ball** in one corner to protect your collection from mites and other predators.

On a label, write the **place** and the **date** you found the insect, also its **name** which you can find out by consulting one of many simple books on insects.

You may wish to store your insects separately if they are large (see above) or in groups (see below), classifying them by species, size, colour, etc.

Collecting shells

a A collection of gastropods. From left to right, top line: limpet; keyhole limpet; cowrie; ormer. Middle line: topshell; sea-snail; whelk; periwinkle. Bottom line: wentletrap; tower shell; cerith; murex; drill.

b A collection of bivalves: From left to right, top line: dog-cockle; ark-shell; lucina; cockle. Middle line: venus; clam; mussel. Bottom line: sunset shell and tellin; oyster; scallop; razor.

How to prepare your shell

It is very easy to find shells when you are on holiday at the seaside. Remember to put them into a sealed plastic bag, with a label showing the **date** and **place** you found them. Then, when you arrive home, you must clean your shells before arranging them.

1. Cleaning the inside of the shells

Here are two very simple methods:

Freezing

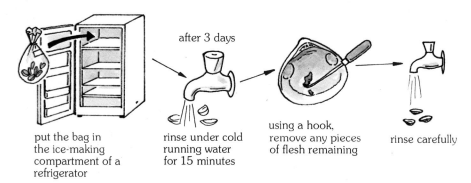

put the bag in the ice-making compartment of a refrigerator

after 3 days

rinse under cold running water for 15 minutes

using a hook, remove any pieces of flesh remaining

rinse carefully

Boiling

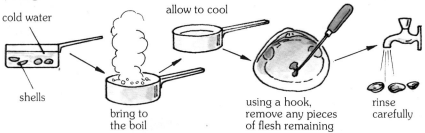

cold water

shells

bring to the boil

allow to cool

using a hook, remove any pieces of flesh remaining

rinse carefully

2. Cleaning the outside of the shells

Often a good **brushing** with a household cleaner will be sufficient.

You can put white shells in a solution of bleach – 5 tablespoonsful of bleach to 1 litre ($1\frac{3}{4}$ pints) of water – for several hours. Always **rinse in plenty of water.**

If the shell has lost its shine because of being rolled around, **rub it care·fully** with a soft cloth and a little vaseline. Never varnish a shell. It would lose all its natural appearance.

3. Arranging your shells

You are now ready to display your shells in a glass case.

If you want them to stand upright, you can stick them gently into a small ball of plasticine or putty (a). Or you can put them into a box with small compartments, like those in which you keep nails or screws.

You can buy one, or make one yourself (b).

Never forget the little label (c and d), giving the **date**, the **place** you found them and the **name** of the creature once you have discovered it. (See pages 15, 18 and 19.)

a

b

c

d

How to classify sea-shells

 If the shell is all in one piece, it is called a univalve or **gastropod**.

If the shell is made up of two halves or valves, it is called a **bivalve** or **lamellibranch**.

Gastropods

Look carefully at the shape, the colour and the markings on the shell. Look at the photographs on page 15 too.

A. Cone-shaped shells

☐ **no hole** at the top . . . . **limpet**

☐ **hole** at the top . . . . **keyhole limpet**

B. Oval shells

☐ like a **coffee bean**, quite small . . . . **cowrie**

☐ like an **ear** . . . . **ormer**

C. Spiral shells

☐ **pearly inside,** pointed top . . . . **top shells**
☐ **not pearly inside** . . . .

– **cone-shaped,** very few coils . . . . **slipper limpet**

– **snail-shaped,** shiny . . . . **sea snail** or
– **elongated**   **necklace**

● large, 7 to 9 cm (2¾ to 3½ in), oval opening . . . . **whelk shell**

● squat, brightly-coloured, 0.5 to 3 cm (³⁄₁₆ to 1 ³⁄₁₆ in) long . . . . **periwinkle**

● broad, vertical ribs . . . . **wentletrap**

● very pointed, numerous coils, spirally ribbed . . . . **tower shell** or **screw shell**

– nobbly . . . . **cerith**

● thick, ridged, grooved, spiny . . . . **drill** and **murex**

Bivalves

Look carefully at the shape, the colour and the markings on the outside of the shell. On the inside, look for the muscle scars and the teeth at the hinge. Look at the photographs on page 15 too.

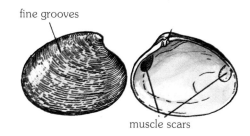

fine grooves

muscle scars

A. The inside of each valve has two clearly defined muscle scars

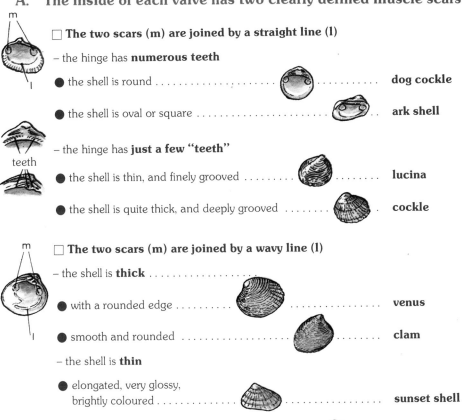

□ **The two scars (m) are joined by a straight line (l)**

– the hinge has **numerous teeth**

● the shell is round . . . . **dog cockle**

● the shell is oval or square . . . . **ark shell**

– the hinge has **just a few "teeth"**

teeth

● the shell is thin, and finely grooved . . . . **lucina**

● the shell is quite thick, and deeply grooved . . . . **cockle**

□ **The two scars (m) are joined by a wavy line (l)**

– the shell is **thick** . . . .

● with a rounded edge . . . . **venus**

● smooth and rounded . . . . **clam**

– the shell is **thin**

● elongated, very glossy, brightly coloured . . . . **sunset shell**

● rounded, often pink . . . . **tellin**

B. The inside of each valve has one clearly defined muscle scar

m

– the shell is very long . . . .  . . . . **razor**

– the shell is pointed at one end and rounded at the other . . . . **mussel**

– the shell is flaky . . . . **oyster**

– the shell is rounded, with straight, fan-like ridges, and wings or "ears" at the hinge . . . . **pecten** or **scallop**

Animal finds

It is not always easy to see live animals in the country, even if you keep your eyes open. Wild animals run away very quickly and know how to keep out of sight. Fortunately, however, there are many animals which leave behind things which tell us something about their way of life. You can look for these things, and find out what animal they might have belonged to and what part they played in the life of the animal.

Nests
Many insects build nests in which to lay their eggs, and these nests are often beautifully constructed. Look at the wasp nests in the photograph (a).

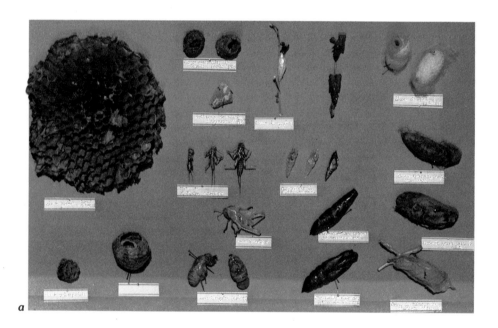

a

Skins and feathers
During the course of their lives **insects'** bodies undergo many changes. As some of them grow, the outer skeleton becomes too small, and a new one grows in its place. The old skin is shed, and left behind. If you find one of these, you can take it home and dry it. You may also find empty cocoons and chrysalises.
Snakes change their skin every year too, while **birds** renew their feathers (b).

b

c

Remains of meals

You will often find partially eaten fruit or empty shells as you walk through the woods or down a country lane. They have been eaten by some creature or another. Nuts and pine-cones are favourite foods of **rodents** such as the squirrel, fieldmouse or rat, and also of birds such as the woodpecker, nut-hatch, magpie and jackdaw.

It is also very easy to find **pellets** (c) which some birds (owls, crows, gulls, etc.) regurgitate two or three times a day. This is a completely natural process; it is the way these birds get rid of the indigestible parts of their food.

d

Bones

Animal bones

You may also find **animal bones** as you walk in the countryside. Most often they will be skull or leg bones.

These bones may be kept **without any special preparation**: it is enough to boil them for a few minutes in water to which a little bleach has been added.

You could try to find out **which group of animals** the bones belonged to.

It is not difficult to distinguish between the two types of skull most frequently found: those of **rodents**, and those of **carnivores**.

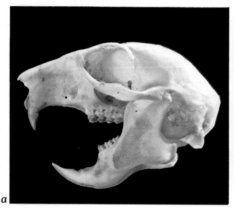

a

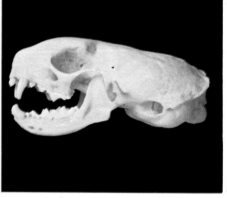

b

In rodents, the jaws have long incisor teeth, but never any canine teeth.

In carnivores, the molars are pointed, and the canine teeth are long and hooked.

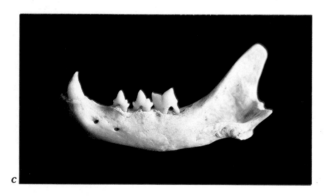

c

A small part of the skull (like that in photograph c) can also be identified. Compare it with the two photographs above. Identification is more difficult with other kinds of bone.

Mounting bones

After eating rabbit or chicken, you could keep the bones, and try to put them together: those which belonged to one leg, for example.

Cleaning

– Boil some water and add some strong washing powder: about one tablespoonful to 2 litres (3½ pints). Put in the bones, and boil for half an hour. Leave to cool.

– Rinse·in clean water and gently scrape off any flesh which remains.

– Put the bones in another saucepan of water together with some bleach: 5 to 6 tablespoonsful to 1 litre (1¾ pints) of water. Boil for a few minutes and allow to cool.

– Dry the bones.

Mounting

Re-assemble the joints. Use a photograph or a drawing to help you.

Stick the bones on to a black background. They will make a very beautiful and interesting collection.

(d and e)–wing and foot of a chicken; (f and g)–front and back legs of a rabbit.

d

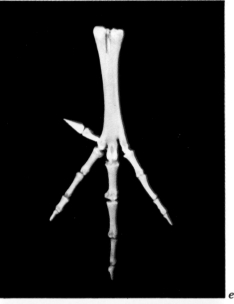

e

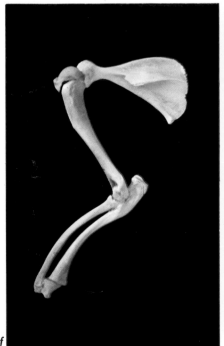

f

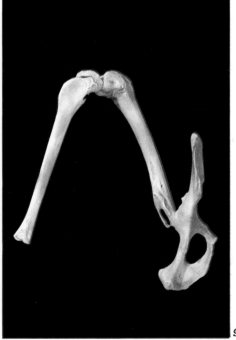

g

Fossils

It is very exciting to find fossils in the ground. They show us examples of plants and animals which were alive millions of years ago. Fossils, like rocks and minerals, belong to everyone, so treat the site with respect. Do not remove more than one or two specimens. It is better to take photographs. When you get home you can make casts of your fossils. And you can enlarge your collection by borrowing fossils from your friends, and making casts of those too.

Different kinds of animal fossils

– Skeleton with **star-like pattern of grooves.** It may be found alone (a) or in a colony (b) . . . . **corals**

– Shell with two valves. One of the valves has an elongated **"beak" with a hole in it.**
(a "foot" used to emerge from this hole to anchor the animal to its support) . . . . **brachiopod**

– Shell with **two halves hinged** at the upper end. There are **muscle scars** on the inside (see page 19) . . . . **bivalve or lamellibranch**

– Shell made **all in one piece,** and usually **coiled in a spiral** . . . . **gastropod**

– Shell made **all in one piece**. May or may not be coiled. Closed by a membrane . . . . **ammonite/ belemnite**

– Body **divided into three** . . . . **trilobite**

– Chalky skeleton. Radially symmetrical . . . . **echinoderm**

–.**Bones** – fish bones or mammal bones . . . . **vertebrate**

a   b

A collection of fossils. From left to right, top line: corals; brachiopods; bivalves; gastropods. Bottom line: belemnites and ammonites; echinoderms; trilobite.

Classifying fossils

You can classify your collection by reference to the place where the items were found. For example, the fossils you can see in the photograph (a) on page 24 were all found in one area.

The age of fossils

Some creatures which we find in fossil form **still exist today**. Compare the actual shells on page 15 with fossil shells. Others, such as trilobites, are only found in primary or palaeozoic sites; while ammonites are only found in secondary or mesozoic sites. Species like this have **completely disappeared**. Fossils help us to understand **how life developed on earth**.

Here are some very broad divisions of time which will help you to identify these distant periods in the history of the world in relation to ourselves. But if you want to classify your fossils according to age, you must consult an expert.

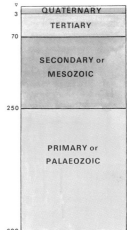

GEOLOGICAL TIME

MILLIONS OF YEARS AGO	
3	QUATERNARY
70	TERTIARY
250	SECONDARY or MESOZOIC
600	PRIMARY or PALAEOZOIC

MILLIONS OF YEARS AGO

c

Rocks and minerals

You may sometimes pick up interesting stones along an embankment, on a mountain path, or in the bed of a stream. (**Do not venture into a tunnel or quarry without permission;** there may be danger of a rock fall.)

Collect freshly broken pieces of stone, or break a small piece off the rock with the help of a small hammer. Always treat the site with respect.

Rocks, minerals or crystals?

Rocks: granite and limestone are rocks. Rocks make up the crust of the Earth, and you can see this substratum quite easily in a quarry. Rocks are not necessarily visible on the surface of the ground, but may be covered by a layer of **soil** of varying thickness, in which plants can grow.

Granite rocks ➜

Minerals: quartz and mica are minerals. **Rocks are made up of all sorts of minerals** packed solidly one against the other, as you can see in this close-up of a piece of granite. There are about 2,500 types of mineral.

Crystals: if the mineral has developed **a precise, geometrical form,** we say it has crystalized.   Crystals may be quite big and occur in isolation, like quartz (see page 30), but more often they are small and mixed in with lots of others, as in granite.

If the mineral does not crystalize, it takes the form of very hard paste (as with the solidified lavas: see basalt on page 29).

You can have fun by making crystals out of salt. Dissolve 35 g ($1\frac{1}{4}$ oz) of cooking salt in 1 litre ($1\frac{3}{4}$ pints) of fresh water. Pour the solution on to a dish and allow it to evaporate slowly. You will see some crystals in a few days' time.

Ores: If a rock contains a large quantity of a mineral which can be used in industry, we say the rock is an **ore**.

How to arrange your rocks

There are several possible ways:

Make a collection of the rocks in your own area

Label each specimen with its name (if you know it) and the exact place it was found.

Draw a simple map of your area, and lay the specimens upon it.

Arrange the rocks in groups

– **colour**

– **texture** (granular, flaky?)

– **density** (are specimens of the same size lighter or heavier than each other?)

– **hardness** (can you scratch the rock with your finger-nail, or a piece of glass, or a steel blade?)

Alongside each rock in your collection, try and put a photograph of the place it was found, as in the example below. Specimen (a) is a piece of red sandstone, and specimen (b) is a type of lava called rhyolite.

How to classify rocks

Carefully examine each of your specimens and try and place it in one of the following categories. (A magnifying-glass will be very useful.)

The rock often contains fossils	**Effervesces** when you pour a few drops of vinegar on it (a) . . . . 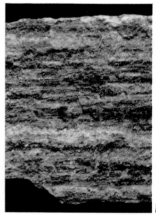VINEGAR	it is **limestone**
	Rock with no visible crystals. Formed from small, tightly-packed grains of sand. **Scratched by glass**	it is **sandstone**
	Soft rock. You can scratch it with your finger nail. Absorbs water	it is **clay**
The rock looks flaky	**Dull-looking rock**	it is **slate**
	Shiny-looking (you can see the mica in it)	it is **mica-schist**
	Rock made up of **many crystals.** You can scratch it with glass (b)	it is **gneiss**
The rock does not contain fossils and does not look flaky	Granular, made up of **many solidly-packed crystals.** You can often see quartz and mica. Can be scratched by glass.	it is **granite**
	Dense rock, very dark in colour. Like a hard paste with no crystals	it is **basalt**
	(All the solidified lavas come into this category.)	

a

b

A collection of rocks.
From left to right:
Top line:
limestone, sandstone, clay.
Middle line:
slate, mica-schist, gneiss.
Bottom line:
granite, basalt.

There are many
types of rock.
— clay, marl, lime-
stone, sandstone
— slate and old sand-
stone
— volcanic rocks (rhy-
olite, basalt)
— granite, gneiss (the
most ancient)

A piece of slate with the imprint of a fern

A piece of marl with an ammonite

Close-up of a piece of basalt

29

How to classify minerals

You will find minerals in the mountains or on mine tips . . .
Always **ask permission** before going on an expedition. Remember! do not take any thing away from a cave.

Minerals are classed according to their chemical composition, and the shape of their crystals. **It is not easy for a beginner**. So try to arrange them according to their colour, their shape, or the place they were found.

Here are a few examples of well-crystalized minerals which should not be too difficult to find:

Rock Salt: It is used in our food. The crystals are transparent, and look like cubes piled one on top of the other.

Fluorine: The crystals are like cubes or pyramids, and vary in colour.

Quartz: Common in mountain areas. It may be white, or yellow, or purple. The crystals are shaped like prisms.

Chalcopyrite: This is a gold-coloured copper ore. It may be found as a round lump or as crystals.

Galena: This is a lead ore, with a bright, metallic shine. It is very dense (even a small piece is very heavy).

Pyrites: This is an iron ore. It often appears as brown crystals. It is common in mica-schist and gneiss.

Gypsum: Used for making plaster. May be fibrous or crystalline.

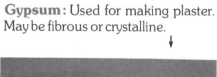

Marcasite: This is another iron ore. It is found in fibrous balls, which are greyish-yellow, and very shiny inside.

Calcite: This ore is found in all the limestone used in building. It is very common, and used to make lime and cement.

Barytes: This is a barium ore, with a lumpy, fibrous texture. Barium is used a great deal in the paint industry.

INDEX